MW01094590

God Moments

in an ordinary life

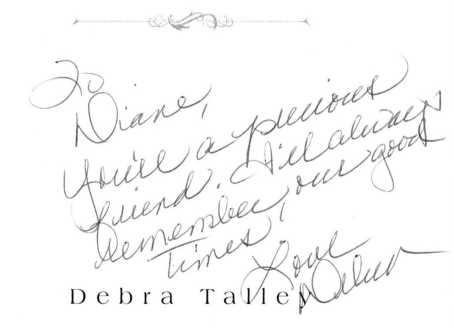

Diane,
You're a precious
friend. I'll always
remember our good
times. Love
Debra

Debra Talley

⬢ dustjacket

Cover Design by Rhonda Minton
Interior Design by D.E. West / DustJacket

Printed in the United States of America

 dustjacket

www.dustjacket.com

"In this moving collection of life experiences Debra Talley shows us that God often speaks in surprising ways. These stories prove how everyday encounters become divine appointments when we simply pause to listen. Debra has learned to see God's hand in situations that most of us are content to overlook. You will be blessed, challenged, and encouraged as you read!"

~ **Dr. Charles F. Stanley**
Senior Pastor, First Baptist Atlanta
Founder and President, In Touch Ministries

I am honored to recommend to you Debra Talley's brand new book. For many years, Debra has encouraged hundreds of thousands through her dedication to the Lord and ministry in music. Debra has inspired mothers and wives across the country and around the world to raise godly children and instill virtue and grace in the next generation. Now she has courageously opened up her heart in the pages of her writing to share the most intimate details of her faith and walk with God. If you are searching for answers and want to be encouraged that God's plans are perfect even when His ways are difficult to understand, you will be blessed by Debra Talley in a brand new way. If you want to read one book this year that will change your perspective and bless your heart this is it.

~ **Matthew Hagee**
Executive Pastor
Cornerstone Church
San Antonio, TX

Debra Talley was practically a newlywed when we began traveling together two hundred days a year on a forty-foot coach. Her new husband, an accomplished musician, had whisked her away to a new town and a new singing family. To many, that sounds like a fantasy life, but in reality there is little privacy living in a bus. I know Debra Talley. I have seen her when her food order was wrong and when she was dissatisfied with her hair before a concert. I have seen her sad at news she received, disappointed and discouraged, but I have never seen her fail to sing her heart out proclaiming the message of

Jesus Christ. You will be blessed, challenged and inspired by Debra's consistent life evident in her writings that give us fresh incentives for survival and practical counsel to implement into the working-out of our faith. Her tender spirit--sensitive to the still small voice of the Father- is obviously the most important work of her day. I cherish calling Debra friend.

~ Connie Hopper
The Hoppers
Gospel Music Hall of Fame Inductee

Thank you, Debra, to alerting us to watch for and be open to *"God Moments"* in our ordinary days. Moments small enough to ignore but big enough to change anything....or everything!

~ Sue Dodge
Gospel Music Icon - Serves with her husband, Amos,
as senior pastors of Capital Church in Vienna, VA

My wife, Roberta, and I have shared our excitement, with Debra, over a new book we had just read several times over the years. She is not only our friend, but our best "book buddy". Now we get to share, with others, our excitement over this book Debra Talley has written.

In a world where so many heroes are spoiled athletes and arrogant stars, Debra has shown us a different kind of hero.....the daycare kids at play, an older lady in a nursing home that most have forgotten, the ones that others walk around and never see. She notices the unnoticed, she sees the unseen, and hears in a simple smile what others can't. She has collected those moments and memories, and like a gift, has put them on paper.

I'm thankful for her voice, her heart, her friendship, and so thankful to have the opportunity to say yes, yes, yes.....to this book!!!!!

~ Aaron Wilburn
Songwriter, Storyteller, & Humorist

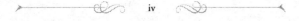

Dedication

To my incredible daughter, Lauren. You inspire me and amaze me. Thank you for all your help and encouragement.

To my wonderful husband, Roger. You've always thought I could do anything. The truth is, I couldn't without you. Thanks for believing in me.

I love you both!

Table of Contents

Foreword

My mother knows everybody in town.

Really, she does. Give her 30 minutes in a store, and she will tell you how many kids the Walmart checkout lady has, or what nursing home the florist's father is in, or that Sheila at the bank just moved here from Pennsylvania. Some are social butterflies; my mom is a social ninja.

I tease her a lot but deep down, I wish I was more like her in that way. She's always interested in the lives of other people and as a result, she has lots of friends. Naturally, every week she has a new story to tell me.

This collection of stories is like a scrapbook for me. Not only are you about to find out all the embarrassing things I did as a child, but I read the stories of familiar people with a whole new perspective. I learn from Miss Minnie that the secret to a long, happy life is in being yourself. I learn from B.J. at the grocery store to be thankful for small things. I learn from a six-year-old version of myself that other people are the best investment there is.

My mom told me recently that when she talks to people and learns about their lives, she feels enriched and gains a sense of purpose for herself. She feels useful and valuable when Kim at the dry cleaners stops to show pictures of her grandkids.

Whoever desires to save his own life will lose it, but whoever loses his life for His sake will find it. When Jesus said that, I think He had my mom in mind. She lives for the God moments in life, the point where blessing others becomes a blessing for us. I hope the moments described in these pages inspire you to look for the God moments at your grocery store, bank, or any of the other seemingly ordinary places life takes you.

(And when my mom strikes up a conversation with you in line, tell her I said hi.)

Lauren Talley Alvey

x

Introduction

Do you ever have seemingly random things happen in your life? You know those unexplained moments in your day that you just didn't see coming? I do almost on a daily basis. I'm a firm believer that there are no coincidences with God and He allows these moments. The more I become aware of Him in my everyday life, the more He reveals to me.

A songwriter friend once told me, when I asked him where he got inspiration for his songs, that he had trained himself to listen to conversations, sermons, stories, anything in his day that might give him an idea for a song.

While preparing the stories for this book, I realized that my friend's words of wisdom have stuck with me on some level. It seems I too have trained myself to listen or at least become more aware of the circumstances and opportunities that God has placed in my path.

Over the years, I have written many short stories from my experiences and I have kept most of these writings for myself to remind me that He is present every moment of every day. Most of the lessons I have learned have come not from eloquent sermons or inspiring books, but from the unexpected moments in my ordinary days. God uses the simplest things to remind me that everyday is an opportunity to experience Him.

As you read about these experiences, observations, and inspirations, I hope you will open your eyes and ears, and especially your heart, to the God Moments in *your* Ordinary Life.

Debra

Bank Prayer Meeting

Ordinary days can sometimes turn into extraordinary days, if we listen to the still small voice that God uses to prompt us to action.

One day, I was doing my errands in town and I decided to go to the bank before an appointment rather than after, as I had originally planned. I finished my business at the teller's window and turned to walk out when I noticed one of the bank officers sitting at her desk, in her office. We often say hello and chat, so when I saw she didn't have a customer with her, I walked over to say good morning. She stopped what she was doing and said, "I saw you walk in a few minutes ago and I wanted to talk to you, but I didn't want to bother you with my problems. I know God sent you over here."

I sat down and asked her how I could help. Tears filled her eyes and she told me her family was going through some very difficult times. After she told me a little bit about their situation and asked if I would remember them in prayer. I assured her that I would. As those words came out of my mouth, I felt that tug in my heart and I knew God wanted me to pray with her right then. "Would it be inappropriate for us to pray right now?" I said. "Not at all," she said, "I pray with my customers whenever I can. I feel God had placed me in this position to witness for Him. I'm just the one that needs prayer now." I thought we would hold hands across her desk, but when I got up to close her door, she was already down on her knees beside her desk. I knelt with her and we prayed.

When we finished, I told her I had something for her that would be an encouragement. I went to my car and got one of my daughter Lauren's new CDs and went back inside to give it to her. When I walked in, she was standing with a tissue box in her hand talking to the tellers. I could hear one of them saying," We didn't know what was wrong." You see, I had closed the door of her office, but I didn't think about the big window that looked out over the bank lobby. The tellers and anyone else in the lobby could see us praying! I gave her the CD, hugged her, and told her I would continue to pray.

As I went on my way, I couldn't help but think about the divine appointment I had just experienced. God is willing to use us, but are we willing to be used? It's so easy to get distracted with the details of our busy lives and think only about ministry moments when they are in the church setting.

I have come to realize that opportunities happen in our everyday lives. If we are open and willing to be used, God never fails to provide those divine appointments.

Crossing Safely

I know traffic lights are a necessity, but I love it when I can sail through them on the green light. An occasional red light isn't a problem. It's time I can use to listen to the radio or check my lipstick, but I didn't expect God to use the short time I was stopped to teach me a lesson.

I was sitting at an intersection one day when I noticed a young man start to cross the four-lane highway. Seeing someone cross at such an intersection on foot is somewhat of an oddity these days. My attention was focused on him for another reason, though. He was using a white cane and was accompanied by another man wearing a bright orange shirt. The man walked slightly behind him at his right elbow. I could see that he was talking to him, as if he were giving him instructions. They continued until they reached the corner. I assumed the man in the orange shirt was teaching the younger man how to get around in his dark world, since the building they were headed for was Volunteer Blind Industries.

It made me think that we as Christians are just like that young man. We are walking through this dark world amid all the hustle, bustle and noise, but God walks every step with us. He is at our

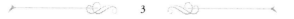

side giving us instructions to navigate the dangerous paths we are sometimes on. If we listen, we will get to the other side safely.

If that young man had not listened to his instructor, he could have gone off course and out into a path that could have left him in a dire situation. However, he listened to the one guiding him and arrived safely. Shouldn't we do the same? We have the Holy Spirit to guide us through every situation we will ever encounter. All we have to do is listen to that still small voice that is guiding us today and we too will arrive safely.

Angel Unaware

God is always putting people in my path to bless me or that I may be a blessing to them. What I have learned is that in each of these situations, God is teaching me how to respond. This is one such lesson on a cold, spring day in Ohio.

It was warm when we left home, so I had packed my spring flip-flops and one pair of sneakers. When we got to Ohio, it was cold and rainy. My feet were cold even with my sneakers on, so I decided I would run into the store and get a pair of socks. As I started to get off the bus, I noticed a small figure about four rows over on the parking lot. It looked like a girl holding a sign facing the entrance to the lot. I stood at the door and watched for a minute or two. No one was even slowing down for her. I couldn't read the sign, but my heart knew what it said. I knew what I had to do. I put twenty dollars in my jacket pocket, got my umbrella, and stepped off the bus.

"How are you doing today?" I called out. She turned toward me and said, "OK, how are you?" As she walked a few steps toward me, I could see her legs were very twisted and she had difficulty walking. She was folding the cardboard sign inward, as if she was embarrassed for me to see it. I told her I had seen her from my bus door and

thought she might be needing some help. "Yes," she said. "I'm a single mom of two and I wouldn't be out here if it weren't for my children." She said, "I have cerebral palsy and I haven't been able to find work. I have benefits coming, but until the benefits start, I need to feed my kids. God has been good to me and I am embarrassed to be out here, but I don't know what else to do." "Well," I said, "I believe God told me to come over and see if I could help you." I started to get the twenty out of my pocket and God said, "You know you have a larger bill folded up in your wallet." Funny, you can't hide a folded up bill from God! You can fold it up tight and even hide it from yourself, but He knows it's there.

I reached into my purse and got the money. As I handed it to her, she began to cry. "I believe God wants me to bless you today and tell you that He has not forgotten you. He knows exactly where you are and what you need," I said. I asked if she was a Christian and she smiled and said yes. I asked if I could pray with her. She grabbed my hands and said, "Yes, please." We bowed our heads and I began to pray, "Dear Lord…" I realized I didn't know her name. "What's your name?" I asked. She looked up at me and said, "Angel." I chuckled and said, "Of course it is!" We continued to pray and when we were finished, I said goodbye. As I walked away, she called out to me, "Hey, I don't know your name." "My name is Debra," I said. "I'll be praying for you too, Debra!" she called back. I walked away with tears rolling down my face.

Skeptics would say that she might have been a con artist and I had been duped. Maybe, but I choose to believe that God puts people in our paths to give us opportunities to not only bless others, but to show God's love in a broken world. For me, it's not important that I know what she did with the money, but it is important that I did what God required of me. Hebrews 13:1-2 says, "Let brotherly love continue. Do not forget to entertain strangers, for by so doing some have unwittingly entertained angels." Angels? Well, at least one Angel that day.

Experiencing God

There are times that we all get discouraged in doing what God has called us to do. We get sort of weary in well doing. Our efforts just don't seem to produce the results we hoped for. We may even take on somewhat of a "God complex" in trying to make things happen, thus the discouragement. It took me over twenty years to fully realize that I can do nothing apart from God. This is a story of how God reminded me that He was still in charge and my issues of discouragement were of my own doing.

The concert started out like any other. All the preparations for the evening had been made. The radio station promoting the benefit event had done an incredible job. The sound was set and the product tables were organized and ready. As the doors opened, we stood behind our product table waiting to greet the people that had begun to come into the large arena. Feeling a bit discouraged, I almost felt a sense of dread. Not that I didn't want to sing for these people, but it just seemed we were going through the motions. That's when God showed up.

One of the first people I spoke with was a lady that told me her husband was a pastor and that he used some of our songs in

their church. She asked for prayer for herself because she had been diagnosed with thyroid cancer and had undergone surgery. The doctors were unable to get all of the cancer cells and she was now facing more surgery. She was using a walker and casually mentioned that she also had MS. It struck me that with all her health issues that she seemed at peace. She asked that I remember her in prayer.

In just a few moments, another lady began to tell me that one of the presidential debates would be held in her town. Since the world would be converging on their small southern town, their church decided they would use the event as an opportunity to reach people for Christ. The church rented every billboard in the city and outside the city limits to display a gospel message without denominational or political affiliations. The church had a local printer make signs to put at businesses and in the yards of people that wanted to help get out the Word. She shared how God had provided the finances to fund this project. Two days after the church had secured the billboards, both political parties had called the sign company to rent them, but God had already given them to the local church for His purpose. She requested prayer for their church and all involved that God would use them for His glory.

The billboard lady had no more finished her story and walked away, when another lady came to me and told me that a young group of girls from the local children's home would be there in just a few minutes. The benefit event was for this children's home and these young ladies were so excited to be able to be there. They had adopted "Orphans of God" as their song and they wanted her to ask if we would sing it that night.

I went to sit in a mostly unoccupied section of seats to listen to the other groups. While I was sitting there, I felt someone touch me on the shoulder. I looked up to see two young girls. They introduced themselves and said they were from the children's home. One of them knelt beside me and told me she had written me a letter, but never mailed it. She went on to say that she was abandoned by her parents and had come to live at the academy. She was thirteen. Since she had been there, "Orphans of God" had become her favorite song. My heart was about to break. I hugged her and assured her we would sing it especially for them.

All the girls from the home sat together in two rows in the back. When we sang "The Broken Ones" early in the program, they all stood with their arms around each other crying. Most of the audience couldn't see them, but I couldn't keep my eyes off of them. After we had done several more songs, Lauren introduced "Orphans of God" and dedicated it to them. When Lauren began the first verse, fifteen young girls spontaneously walked from their seats in the back to the edge of the stage and began to sing with us. It was almost more than I could bear as I watched them stand and sing:

There are no strangers
There are no outcasts
There are no orphans of God

After our set, we met each one of them, gave them signed pictures, hugged them several times, took pictures with them and met their wonderful house parents. I asked for a list of their names so I could pray for them. I still have that list.

After our set, another person shared that our songs had meant so much to her during a very difficult time in her life. Her brother and his entire family had perished in a house fire. Two weeks later, she lost two more family members. She went on to say God had ministered to her through those songs.

During our set I had shared a story about my mother-in-law and her journey through Alzheimer's disease. Afterward, a gentleman came to me with tears in his eyes. He shared with me that he had lost both of his parents to this terrible disease and now he had been diagnosed with Alzheimer's. This dear man said he was uneducated and could neither read nor write, but he was a multimillionaire. He credited God with his blessed life. He said his money could do nothing for him now but provide for his care. He was comforted in the fact he knew that he was going to heaven when his time came.

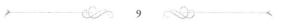

By the end of that night, I was emotionally drained. These were only a few of the stories we heard that night. I say *we* because Lauren had heard story after story from different people. At one point, I looked at her and said, "What is going on here?" She just shook her head and said, "I don't know. Are you hearing what I'm hearing?"

After the concert, Lauren and I were in the bus talking about all of the things that had just taken place. We spent an hour just sharing what each of us had witnessed. What did it all mean? Why that place? Why that night? I can't answer that. All I know is that what started out to be another concert turned into a divine interruption. God brought a deluge to wash away my discouragement. He used each of those people to help me refocus. It was never about me, but all about Him. He had brought peace in chaos, comfort in pain, joy in trials, love in abandonment, and assurance in doubt. He sent each one to let me know that there was no need to be discouraged. He was in control. All I had to do was open my eyes and see Him at work.

God is constantly at work all around us. There are opportunities for us to get in on what He is doing. The answer to discouragement is service. There's an opportunity out there. Don't miss it! God is waiting for you to experience Him!

Paying It Forward

I was taught the Golden Rule as a child, "Do unto others as you would have them do unto you." I have tried to live my life by that principle.

There was a movie some years ago entitled "Pay It Forward." The premise of the movie was that as acts of kindness were shown to the characters they, in turn, touched others by "paying forward" acts of kindness. It was sort of a modern take on The Golden Rule.

Long before "Pay It Forward" was a catch phrase for doing the right thing, I was the recipient of many acts of kindness early in my singing career. There were special people that God put in my path to encourage me. I decided long ago that, because it meant so much to me, encouraging others was something I could do to "pay it forward."

One of the people that demonstrated this principle to me was a man named, Paul Boden. Paul was known in the southern gospel industry as the editor of US Gospel News. Some may not know that Paul traveled for years with various quartets and was a very talented singer. I met Paul when I had first joined the Song Masters Quartet.

I was young, inexperienced at singing (except in church), and lacking confidence. I was hired to fill the position that my bosses' daughter had held in the group. She was a great singer and I, well, was not. I knew that God had placed me there and even though the group was very supportive, I struggled to find my own voice.

One of the first places I sang with them was in Walnut Ridge, Arkansas. Several other groups sang on the program that night and one of the groups was Paul's group. Those guys were good! After the concert, we went to the home of one of the other groups to eat and fellowship.

I knew that night that my performance was not as good as their daughter's would have been, but the other groups were very kind and encouraging. I will never forget when my boss, Joel Kelsey, asked Paul what he thought about their new girl singer. Paul kindly looked at me and said, "I think she will be just fine. Just give her a little time."

It wasn't an overstated compliment. It was just a simple vote of confidence for a young girl who had very little. That one statement gave me the courage to keep trying. Now when I meet young artists, I remember Paul's words to me and I try to give them just a word of encouragement.

Words are very powerful. Their effect can be felt for years. Words can break a person's spirit or they can build confidence and self-esteem. Paul is gone now, but he was one of those people who used his words wisely to make a difference in one young girl's life. His words have stayed with me all these years and I intend to follow his example and pay it forward. Thanks Paul!

Five Dollars and a Little Faith

I hate exercise! I have several unused pieces of exercise equipment to prove it. (Well, that and my mirror.) I don't mind walking, but never seem to commit to a daily regimen. So I'll admit it, I'm out of shape. Just as our physical bodies can be out of shape, so can our spiritual lives. We read our Bibles, pray, listen to sermons, and sing along with the praise and worship team. All of those things are beneficial, but until we *exercise* our faith, we won't grow any spiritual muscle. I began learning about exercising my faith early in my singing career. It all started with a five dollar bill.

When I first started singing professionally, I only made eighty dollars a week. Now, before you feel too sorry for me, that was back in the early seventies. However, that wasn't much money even back then, come to think of it. Thankfully, I didn't have credit cards to fall back on when I was in a bind or I would have really gotten into trouble. I did learn to budget and watch my pennies.

One of the best lessons I ever learned was in church. The Song Masters, the first group I sang with, had sung our first set and sat down on the front pew while the pastor was preparing to take the offering. He explained that the offering would go to missions and

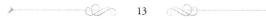

then we bowed our heads while he blessed the offering. While we were praying, God began to speak to my heart about giving in that offering. That's when I stopped listening because I only had five dollars. Let me explain.

As a child, I was taught to tithe, you know, give the first ten percent to God. It *is* His after all. When I got paid each week, my first order of business was to write a check for my tithe. This particular week I had written checks for all my bills, trying to stretch each cent of my meager bank account. When I finished, I realized I only had five dollars left to buy my food on the road for the rest of the week. Food wasn't as expensive then, but there weren't any dollar menus, either. Five dollars wouldn't have gone too far. We depended a lot on the goodness of the churches we sang in. Some would prepare meals for us or we would be invited to church members' homes. We just never knew beforehand if those invitations would be there. At any rate, I didn't go hungry. Most of the time, though, I had more than five dollars left. This time I would just have to make it work.

Back to the prayer for the offering. I was sitting there, minding my own business listening to the pastor pray, when God spoke to me and said, "You have money, put it in the offering." I pretended I didn't hear. The pastor had finished praying and the ushers were passing the offering plates.

God said, "Put the money in the plate."

"I only have five dollars, Lord," I said.

"Put it in," He said.

"But, Lord, I have to eat the rest of the week and five dollars is all I have." Like He didn't know!

Silence. As the plate came closer, I knew what I had to do. I opened my purse, took out the five dollar bill, and put it in as the plate went by. I was concerned about my meal situation, but decided

God wanted that five dollars so He would just have to feed me! I didn't tell anyone in the group about what had happened. I wanted God to be on His own providing for me! I had heard about folks living by faith, but until now, I had never really had to do that. I was about to learn a very valuable lesson.

We left that night heading to our next date. When we left the church, my boss, Joel, asked where everyone wanted to eat. I cringed. I hadn't eaten since noon, but I wasn't about to tell them about my lack of funds. Then Joel said, "A man walked up to me tonight and gave me money to buy us all dinner." That sort of thing happened on occasion, but I gave God credit for timing. I ate as much as I could, just in case my next meal was further down the road.

The next day we sang at a church that we had been to before and knew some of the people. One of the families asked us to their home for a meal. That night someone else provided dinner for us after the concert and so it went for three days. By now, I was beginning to be a little impressed with God and my faith was increasing daily. Each time a meal was prepared for us, I would thank God for His provision. Still, I didn't tell anyone about my situation. God had fed me all week and my empty wallet wasn't even on my mind.

On Saturday, our concert was in southern Illinois in an old theater. We had been to a couple of the churches in the area, so we were looking forward to seeing some people we knew. I had stayed with a wonderful family, the Brownings, during a week-long revival and hadn't seen them in a year or so. I hoped they would be there so we could catch up. I was behind our product table when I saw them walk in. They came over and we exchanged hugs. While we were chatting, Mrs. Browning took my hand discreetly and put something in it. I didn't look right then. I thought it might be a note or something from one of her kids or a song request. I thanked her and went back to the table and they went in the auditorium. Back behind one of the album racks, I looked to see what she had placed there. As I opened my hand, I saw green! The whole week of God

supplying my need passed before my eyes and my faith soared. He had been so faithful. Should I be so bold to think that He was also returning my five dollars? I opened the folded bill and I couldn't believe my eyes. There in my shaking hand was a one hundred dollar bill!! God had blessed me twenty-fold!

There have been many times over the years that I have heard God's voice about giving. When I hesitate even for an instant, He reminds me of this time in my life. The Word says that if we have faith the size of a mustard seed we can move mountains. I'm not sure my faith in the beginning was even that size, but God was teaching me and growing my faith by showing me how He works when I obey.

Exercise. Still not my favorite thing. God's faith-building exercise, now there's a plan I can follow.

...By the Seat of His Pants

Anyone that travels, as I have for years, could write volumes about the things that happen on the road. Some experiences are difficult and you would just as soon forget. Then there are some experiences that are just plain funny and you laugh no matter how many times they come to mind. This is one of the funniest things that I have ever witnessed.

The first group I was with, the Song Masters, was singing in Dyersburg, Tennessee, for a revival meeting. It was their home church and the church was packed that night. One of the friends in the audience was a precious man everyone called Pop Webb. Pop had been saved under the Song Masters' ministry at the age of seventy. He became a devoted fan and would always be in the crowd when they were in the area singing. His favorite song was the Laverne Tripp song, "I Know, I Know." He would shout every time he heard the song. Having come to Christ at a late age, he said he was making up for lost time.

We started the service that night and the crowd was with us from the start. Hands were clapping and "Amen" and "Praise the Lord" could be heard throughout the church. After we had sung several songs and Joel Kelsey, our leader, had done a little spontaneous preaching, we launched into Pop's favorite song. He was all smiles and hallelujahs. You could see he was getting blessed and you knew what was coming next. Let's pause here before I continue with the story and let me describe Pop Webb a little so you can get the full picture.

Pop was only five feet five inches at the most. I know because with heels on, I was taller. He was almost as round as he was tall, balding, and he wore his trousers up over his little round tummy. Picture the Pillsbury Doughboy at 74 and in church and you've got the right image.

Back to the story. We sang two verses back to back and we could see Pop was about to, well, *pop*! When we got to the chorus, "I know, I know, there's no doubt about it. He lives in my heart and I'm gonna shout it," he couldn't stay seated any longer. He jumped to his feet and pumped his little short arm in the air and shouted, "Hallelujah," "Praise the Lord!" Each time he would do this his little tummy would jump. About the fourth time he inhaled to shout, "Praise the Lord," his trousers fell to his feet!

We were all shocked. The crowd began to realize what had happened. Laughter started on the front row and went like a wave to the back. The pastor was laughing and beating on the arm of his chair. The minister of music was laughing so hard he dropped to his knees in front of the pew where he had been sitting. We couldn't believe it, but as any good gospel group would do, we kept singing. Joel looked toward me and Dale, our lead singer, and said, "Don't you dare stop!" We didn't stop and neither did Pop Webb. He heart was so full, his trousers dropping didn't faze him. He picked them up and kept shouting!

Really, what can you do to follow that? The pastor wasn't about to try to preach, so he did what any good Baptist preacher would do. He took an offering. As folks were trying to get control over their laughter, he stood up and said, "Folks, I think we need to take this offering for Pop Webb. We need to buy him some boxers that say 'Praise The Lord' across the seat!"

Pop is gone now, but I have a feeling that somewhere, in heaven, he's still shouting.

His Strength is Perfect

There are some people that you never forget, especially when God uses them to teach you a lesson.

A few years ago, I was teaching at the Steve Hurst School of Music, a week-long camp for singers and musicians. One afternoon I had a very special encounter.

It was one of my last lessons for the afternoon and I was very tired and ready for the day to end. A red-haired young man, about sixteen, walked into my studio for a voice lesson. He introduced himself as Corey. He explained that he had come with a group from his church and that he really wasn't a singer, but his mom had insisted he take voice lessons.

He seemed very shy and nervous and reluctant to even be there. As we talked, I detected a very pronounced speech impediment. I told him he didn't have to sing if he didn't want to. We talked for a few minutes and he seemed to relax a bit. I asked him about himself and why he had come to the school. He said he knew Steve and that he had encouraged him to come to the school. I suspected Steve may have wanted to help him overcome his shyness and suggested Corey take one of the courses of study.

There was something so special about this timid young man. I couldn't quite put my finger on it, but silently I began to pray that God would help me to say something to him that would help him in some way. Although he said he didn't want to sing for me, I asked him what his favorite song was. He said, "Do you know the song His Strength Is Perfect?" I told him I knew the song and I loved it! Then he said very shyly, "I guess I could sing a little of it for you." I told him I would love to hear him sing it. Corey closed his eyes and began to sing:

> *His strength is perfect when our strength is gone*
> *He'll carry us when we can't carry on*
> *Made in his likeness the weak become strong*
> *His strength is perfect His strength is perfect!*

Even though his voice wasn't the best and his speech impediment was present on every line, it was one of the most beautiful things I had ever heard. Tears flowed down my face as I listened and experienced a sweet, gentle spirit in the room. God began to show me, through this young man, that none of us is perfect and he delights in taking our weaknesses and working through them for His glory. I knew at that moment that God was going to use Corey in a very special way. Maybe he wasn't a great singer, but what if the next Billy Graham was standing in front of me?

Ten years later, I received e-mail from Corey asking if I remembered him from the school. Of course, I remembered. I'll never forget him. He is now, on staff, serving God at a church in Oklahoma. I'm not sure Corey learned anything that day from me, but I learned a great lesson from him.

The weaknesses in my life are the very things that God values. When I trust him with what I cannot do, His strength is made perfect in my weakness.

Pride and a Red Walker

I am an independent and self-sufficient person. Like a lot of firstborn children, I want to be in control of things and not rely on others too much. I'm the one that should be able to handle things. Right? Wrong. This is the story of a lesson I learned about pride.

A few years ago, I had some minor surgery on both feet. I had been trying to be patient and stay off my feet, as the doctor ordered, to help the healing process. The downtime was supposed to be at least three weeks. Ugh! This should have been a welcomed respite, but I found I wanted the ordeal to be over and done with and it had only been four days!

Upon learning of my surgery, our secretary, Bobbie, offered to loan me a walker to help me get around while I was recuperating. The offer was very thoughtful and caring of her, but I was sure *I* would not need it. After all, walkers are for old people, aren't they? Wrong again! By the second day, I decided the walker was a great idea. She brought in a sporty red walker with a seat and hand brake. All it needed was a horn and a bell! If I was going to have to hobble around, I might as well do it in style.

My family was great to help with the routine chores and even waited on me for a couple of days, but they just couldn't do everything for me. You know what I mean? When I needed to "go," I just didn't have time to wait on them to get to me to walk me to the bathroom. That's when I swallowed my pride and that sporty walker became my friend.

It took a couple of weeks to get back on my feet and I still needed help for the rest of my recovery. It had never occurred to me that my self-sufficient nature could just be pride. The experience taught me a lesson in humility and was a reminder of my prideful nature.

How could I say I completely trusted God, when my pride got in the way of something as simple as leaning on others for personal needs after surgery and thinking I didn't need the walker, even though I did?

Pride is mentioned many times in the Bible. Pride indicates that one is self-sufficient, doing things as he/she thinks best, and relying on one's own devices and understanding. Proverbs 3:5 says, "Trust in the Lord with all thine heart; and lean not unto thine own understanding. In all thy ways acknowledge Him, and He shall direct thy paths."

I'm thankful that God is patient and continues to teach me about trust. I acknowledge that I can't do anything without Him and He will direct my path, even when I'm walking it with a sporty red walker!

Worry vs. Trust

When you realize the magnitude of the situations that so many people face, it can make you feel helpless and hopeless. I know, I have felt that too. Isn't that what the enemy wants us to feel? God has shown me over and over again that He has not changed. We can't rely on how we feel, but on what His word says. Malachi 3:6 says, "I am the Lord, I change not."

It seems that daily we see drastic changes all around us, the stock market crisis, homeowners not being able to pay their mortgages, jobs ending unexpectedly, prices rising, businesses closing, families faced with illness, even death, the list seems endless. Yet the Word says, "Look at the birds of the air, for they neither sow nor reap nor gather into barns, yet your heavenly Father feeds them. Are *you* not of more value than they?" (Matthew 6:26)

We can worry about tomorrow, even though we can't do a thing about it, or we can trust God. A few years ago, I saw a sign on a church bulletin board that said, "You can't worry and trust at the same time." Worry and trust are opposites. Worry is futile. Trust is hopeful. Hope in our own abilities? No, hope in the Lord and trust in His faithfulness.

Since we don't have the answers, why not cast your cares on Him and see what He will do? It is when things look impossible that He delights in showing us Himself and His power. Cast all your cares on Him, for He cares for you!

No Language Barrier

The one thing I always come away with when we travel out of the country is that no matter where we go, we are all the same. Our customs, traditions, and food may be different, but human beings are the same. The issues that we face in life are global.

We were on a ten day trip to Norway, singing in several cities. Our hosts, Aud and Johan Halsne, are dear friends and Godly people with servants' hearts. During a prayer time with our friends, before the concert one night, I realized that we were praying together in our different languages. It made me smile.

God didn't have any problem understanding any of us, as we prayed at the same time. We in English, they in Norwegian. No interpreter was needed because prayer is a heavenly language. The only barriers are the ones we erect by not talking to our Heavenly Father.

Whether our prayers are in a different language, beautifully crafted words, or just a simple cry of the heart, God hears each one. The only prayer that is not heard is the one we never pray. Whatever your prayer is today, be assured God hears each one.

Does He Care?

My mother-in-law was diagnosed with Alzheimer's disease in 2000. She was one of the Godliest and most sweet-spirited ladies you would ever want to meet. She displayed the heart of a servant and was loved by everyone that knew her.

I will admit that, before she was diagnosed, I feared having someone close to me be stricken with this cruel disease. The day we got the final word from the psychologist that it was what we had suspected, I was devastated. I remember leaving the doctor's office and driving to the mall parking lot, where I had a good cry. It just didn't seem fair that someone like my sweet mother-in-law should have this horrid disease. Some people would be more spiritual than I and could say "thy will be done." I just couldn't say that at that moment. I was angry and scared and I figured God knew it anyway, so I just told Him how I felt. I told Him that she was a good person, a servant, and a godly woman and that she didn't deserve this. I reminded Him of all the evil people in the world and if I were Him, I would give this disease to them. That would be justice, wouldn't it? (Aren't we all glad that I'm not God!) I poured out my heart for about a half an hour. I didn't get any answers right then. Maybe because I was doing all the talking and He couldn't get a word in.

So, I started my car and headed home. In my heart, I knew God was in control and would be with us through this, but my heart still ached and I needed comfort and answers.

While driving home, I continued to pray. I told God that *if* He was with us and *if* He really cared, I needed to hear from Him right away! My prayer may have seemed a bit disrespectful. Even bossy. I didn't mean it that way. It was earnest cry for help from my Father.

When I got home, I went upstairs and picked up a devotional Bible on the nightstand. Sitting on the bedside, I opened the Bible. I could hardly believe my eyes. It had fallen open to a devotional page and the first line said, "My wife has Alzheimer's." The story was from a professor that was caring for his wife. He told of the many times God had taken care of them and had helped them meet the challenges of this disease. His final statement was that he wouldn't trade these years for anything because they had been some of the sweetest years of their marriage. I began to weep and thank God. He did care! He cared enough to let me be angry and hurt and then give me exactly what I had asked of Him.

I believe the message of that story was God letting me know this wouldn't be easy, but we would still have sweet moments with our loved one that would be preserved in our memories for the difficult times.

God is our Father and He wants to help his children. Even when we are hurt and angry, He is loving and kind and wants to meet our needs. Whatever you may be facing, our Father wants to help you, hold you, and bring you through the darkest trial. There is an old song, that I love, titled "Does Jesus Care?" I can say, from experience, He definitely does!

Praying to Play

I've always wanted to play the piano. I took five years of piano lessons when I was a kid. One of my piano teachers was also my mom's first piano teacher. Since I didn't commit myself to really working at it, I can't play. My mom, on the other hand, has played her whole life. She became the church pianist when she was fifteen years old and she held that position over sixty years.

My mom didn't like the lessons either and quit after a couple of months. Her problem was she wanted to play what she heard in her head and the discipline of learning and studying theory was frustrating to her. Mom can read music a little, but she plays five instruments by ear.

One day my mother and I were talking about playing and I told her I regretted not being more serious about the piano. I asked her how she became the church pianist at such a young age, when she really hadn't studied at all. The story she told me left me in awe.

Mom was raised by her grandparents and they took her to church, where she became best friends with the pastor's daughter. She and several of the young girls loved spending Sunday afternoons

together. One of the couples in that church didn't have children of their own, but they loved to have kids from the church come for Sunday dinner. Sister Bugg, as she was called, was a wonderful cook, so Mom and her friends would often invite themselves home for Sunday dinner if the couple didn't ask them first.

As mom recalls, one Sunday all the girls went home with the Buggs for dinner. While the other girls were in the kitchen helping, Mom sneaked off to the parlor, where the piano was. She was trying to play a song and was getting very frustrated that she couldn't play the chords she heard in her head. She stopped playing, bowed her head and said, "Lord, if you will let me play what I hear in my head, I will always play for you." She said that, at that moment, she put her hands on the keyboard and began to play all the chords that she was not able to play before. She couldn't explain it, but her hands just moved across the keys as never before. In Mom's words, "I *know* the Lord touched me that day."

She became the church pianist. Her best friend, the pastor's daughter, learned to play by the music and they played together for many years. Mom still loves to play and by others' accounts, they can't do without her.

How does such a thing happen? Only God knows. God knew that a small church congregation needed a pianist. He knew He had given a measure of talent and a desire to play to a young girl. When she called out to him for help and committed her talent and her life to serving Him, He answered in a supernatural way.

I can only imagine the smile on God's face that day as he took pleasure in answering the prayer of a young girl. After sixty-plus years, she's still playing and I believe He's still smiling.

Purpose Driven Mom

My mom is one of a kind. She's only five feet tall…well, almost, but she's a giant when it comes to love and caring. I've never known anyone with more dedication and commitment to their family and to the Lord.

My mom has served the Lord and the church I grew up in for over sixty years as their pianist. We couldn't miss church growing up. Every time the doors were open, we were there. Mom played the piano and Dad taught Sunday school, so the only time we would miss was if we were really, really sick.

Mom played for the congregational singing and anyone who was asked to sing, as we called it then, a "special." Many times a visitor would be asked to sing and they would have no accompaniment, so our song leader, would volunteer Mom's services at the piano. Sometimes they would want to sing a song Mom hadn't heard. She would tell them to just start singing and she would find the key they were in and by the time they got a few words into the song, she was following them. It was always a marvel to me that she could play anything she heard. (That's another story.)

What impressed me even more was that she never complained. Even though she worked a full-time job at a factory and had a husband and four children to take care of, she was always faithful. Four times a week and anytime there was a revival or special service, she was there.

A few years ago, I was visiting my mom and dad on a weekend. Since they both had obligations at church, they needed to be there early. I told them I would wait until they had finished getting ready and then I would get ready and meet them at the church for the worship service. That's when my mom shocked me as she announced she wasn't going to Sunday school. What?!

I told her she didn't need to miss on my account. She said, "I'm not. I haven't been going to my Sunday School class for a few weeks. I go, but I just help in the church office until the worship service starts." I was dumbfounded. We never missed any part of church. "Why aren't you going to your class?" I asked. "Well, they're doing one of those *studies*," she answered. I asked what study they were doing and she replied, "Oh, it's that Purpose Driven Life." I told her that I had read the book and I thought it was really good. She said, "Oh, I read the book. You're right, it's real good." I said, "Then why don't you go?" She replied, very humbly, "I just don't need it. I've always known what my purpose was. My purpose was to be on that piano bench."

I was speechless. There was no arguing that point. God had revealed to her at as a young girl what her purpose and calling was. Going through a study wasn't going to define it any further for her. I've mulled that over in my mind many times. How many people are looking for purpose in their lives? Time and money are wasted trying to find what makes them feel fulfilled. Promotions, relationships, possessions, wealth, and status are just a few of the things that distract us. When those things are achieved, we realize that we are still not fulfilled. Temporal things are just no substitute for the Divine.

God has a specific plan and purpose for each life. He has a job for each of us to do. Just ask my Mom.

God Moments in an Ordinary Life

The Missionary and the Bass Fiddle

I expect to receive a blessing when I'm at church. The pastor's sermon is what I wait for. God always has something for me to learn. However, this particular Sunday, the lesson God had for me started in the orchestra.

There was a good crowd at church that Sunday. So good, we had to sit in the balcony. From our vantage point, we could see the entire choir, orchestra, and pulpit area. During the worship portion of the service, my eyes were drawn to the orchestra. The orchestra was small that day and one man stood out to me.

He was an elderly gentleman playing the bass fiddle on the right side of the stage. He played with skill and dedication. The notes he played didn't stand out, but he blended with the other instruments to create beautiful accompaniment for the choir and congregation singing.

I realized I had seen him before. I had heard him speak during the Christmas holidays, when he was asked to give a testimony for the Lottie Moon missions offering. He was called upon once again to speak to the congregation.

This dear man had been a missionary for over 40 years. He spoke about how much the support of the local churches had meant to him and his wife all the years they had been on the mission field. His speech was filled with passion, as if he were delivering one of his sermons from those days. He finished and walked back to his place in the orchestra, where he now serves.

He could be traveling around now and speaking to crowds about missions and be applauded for his service to God, but he uses his gifts now to serve the Lord in the local church. He is still ministering, even though he is no longer on the mission field.

To minister means to serve. Service isn't about being in the spotlight, but it's about obedience to the call of Christ and letting His light shine through you as you serve others.

A person in the spotlight can only see to where the spotlight ends. If he or she walks out of the light, there is darkness and danger of falling. But the light of Christ, in us, shines for all to see and follow. Matthew 5:16 says "Let your light so shine before men, that they may see your good works and glorify your Father in heaven."

When the light shines on us, we are glorified. When His light shines from within us, the Father is glorified. What has God called you to do?

Soprano Heart

One of my favorite songs that we've ever sung is a medley of two classic songs, "Shout To The Lord" and "How Great Thou Art." Roger and Lauren arranged the two songs to create a powerful moment in our concerts. Each time we sing it, I am deeply moved.

There's a part of me that wishes that I was a soprano. Don't we always want what we don't have? I wanted a high voice that could build a song to lofty heights and end on a magnificent soaring note, but that's not me!

While this medley was being arranged, I envisioned a Julie Andrews, "Sound of Music", mountaintop moment singing "How Great Thou Art" to God. I'm not sure I could twirl around and sing at the same time!

That voice is only in my dreams, but my heart soars just the same. Each time we sing, "Then sings my soul, my Savior God to thee, how great thou art," I am overwhelmed with gratitude for who He is and what He has done for me. It is incomprehensible that the creator of the universe, Almighty God, lives within me.

Our voices may all be different, but the collective praise and worship is beautiful music to God's ears. Even though my voice has limitations, my soprano heart will "Shout To The Lord…How Great Thou Art!"

I'm Just Me

The elderly lady was lying in her bed in the nursing home. Cancer had invaded her frail little body and her family had been given the sad news that she had only three or four months to live. Since some of her children lived some distance away from the nursing home where she was in our town, a friend gave me her name and thought I might be able to go and visit her. I gently tapped on her door and entered her room. As I went to her bedside I said, "Are you Miss Minnie?"

She smiled and said in a weak little voice, "Yes, I am." I told her who I was and that I knew one of her sons. That started our conversation about her children. She told me where each one lived and what they did. One of her sons is quite successful in music and I asked her where all his musical talent came from. She said, "Well, his father's side claims it, but I remember my grandfather playing the banjo for us kids." "Well, they can't take all the credit, can they?" I said. She just laughed and said, "No, I don't think so."

After we had talked a few minutes, I said, "I hope I'm not disturbing you. I noticed you were watching Matlock when I came in." She said, "Oh no, you're not disturbing me. I do like Andy

Griffith. There's just nothing on now that's good. I still like the old shows…I guess because I'm old." I said, "May I ask how old you are?" She proudly said, "I'm ninety-six." I asked her what her secret was for living such a long time. I was expecting her to say something about her faith or her diet or some sage advice. She looked away for a second, thinking about her answer. After she pondered for just a moment, she humbly said, "I don't have a secret. I'm just me."

"Well, apparently, that's served you well," I said. After a little more conversation, I asked her if I could pray with her. She said, "Oh, I would love that." We prayed and I gave her a hug and told her I would be back to see her.

As I left the building, I kept thinking about her saying, "I'm just me." Many of us are not content being who we are…the person God made us to be. Some strive for fame, fortune, acceptance, and possessions. When in the end, none of that matters. The people in our lives, the God we serve, and the way we live this life make up the sum of who we are. Miss Minnie knows that. Her ninety-six years are proof of it.

I may not make it to ninety-six, only God knows. What I do know is that I want to live life in the present, loving God, enjoying my family, and holding my possessions in an open hand, and hopefully making a difference in someone's life. If I'm able to do those things with my life, maybe I'll be able to say like Miss Minnie, "I'm just me."

K-Mart and Comforters

The best part of any week is Wednesday, the day I visit Miss Minnie. During Easter week I thought I would get Miss Minnie an Easter lily for her room at the nursing home. What started as an invitation from a friend to just check in on her has turned into a wonderful friendship for me.

She's ninety-six, her body is failing, but her mind is sharp. Miss Minnie talks to me about her family, her childhood, what it was like in the early 1900's. We talk about cooking, flowers, and the Lord. She is frail, but a little feisty. She has started joking with me a little now and it makes my day to see that twinkle in her eye. She likes music, birds, flowers, and butter pecan ice cream. My kind of girl! Her life was hard, but there is never a complaint. A gentle, sweet, humble spirit welcomes me each time I enter her room.

While driving to the nursing home, I thought about how beautiful the day was and I wished I could take Miss Minnie into the courtyard for some sunshine, but it was too cool and I wasn't sure she would be up to it. I wished I could take spring to her. Then the thought hit me: *the comforter on her bed is well worn. There's a store right on the way, I'll check there.* Pulling in to the K-Mart parking lot

 43

I prayed, "Lord, would you let there be a beautiful spring-looking comforter that would be just right and Lord, I'd like to have it for twenty dollars." I wasn't trying to be cheap, I only had about forty dollars with me that day.

A whole row of comforters on my left were just not what I was looking for. They were too dark, too geometric, too…well, *ugly*. As I started down the next aisle, there it was, practically leaping off the shelf: white, with birds and flowering branches in spring blues, greens, and yellows. Perfect! At that point, I didn't care what it cost, it was going to be Miss Minnie's. Then I spotted that little yellow sale sticker. The price was so faded I thought my eyes were failing. My heart skipped a beat. (That happens when ladies find a sale.) Twenty dollars, you're thinking? Nope. It was sixteen dollars! I couldn't believe it. A beautiful, reversible comforter for sixteen dollars! I had enough left to buy her a potted flower. God really does love to show off, doesn't he? I made my purchase and drove to the nursing home with a smile on my face.

I buzzed in at the front door of the nursing home, checked in and started down the hallway with an Easter lily and a comforter. Spring had marched in the door and was headed to room 325 and was about to move in with Miss Minnie. I was just carrying its bags.

When I got to the room, the aides were attending to Miss Minnie, so I waited outside the door. They left and I walked in carrying Spring. When I gave her the flower and showed her the comforter, she was excited. "Would you put it on my bed?" she said. "Of course I will," I said. She began to rub her hand over the flowery pattern. "Oh it's so pretty and it has birds! Now I can imagine them singing!" As I choked back tears, she said, "Can I hug you?" Those frail little arms wrapped around me as I bent close. I hope God liked that hug, because it was for Him, not me. I sure did enjoy it, though.

When I first walked in, I saw that Miss Minnie had a new roommate. She introduced me to Janice and we had a nice visit.

Janice said how beautiful Miss Minnie's comforter was and jokingly said Miss Minnie better keep her eye on it or it might wind up on her bed.

I stayed about an hour and when it was time to go, I told Janice that Minnie and I always pray together and asked if she would like to join us. "Yes, I would love that," she said. We held hands and I prayed. When the prayer was finished, I looked up and Janice was crying. I put my arms around her and she looked up at me with tears running down her face and said, "Thank you so much. I need that." As Janice wiped her eyes, I looked at Minnie and she said so softly and with such compassion, "She felt the Spirit." After a moment or two, I said my goodbyes and told them I would be back next Wednesday.

I got into my car and started down the road thinking about what I had just experienced. As I neared K-Mart, where I had just been, the Lord said, "I gave you what you asked for. You have money left. Go buy Janice a comforter." I went back in and found a beautiful light blue striped comforter for, yes, sixteen dollars and I had money left over to buy another flower. My purchases complete, I headed back to the nursing home. I started back down the hall to their room. One of the nurses that had seen me the first time said, "Well here you are again. Are you decorating the whole place today?!" I laughed and said, "No, just one room," and kept walking.

When I got to the door, they looked surprised to see me and thought I had left something I said, "No, I just thought Janice needed a little spring too." I put her potted plant on her table and told her she would need to give it a drink when it got dry. I asked her if she liked the comforter even though it was different from Minnie's. She said, "Oh, yes I love it and it's blue." Apparently, a favorite color of hers. As I was putting the comforter on for her, I teased them saying, "Now I got different ones for you girls, 'cause I didn't want you fighting in here!" We had a big laugh and they assured me they wouldn't, but that everyone would be jealous of them!

For the second time, I said my goodbyes. As I walked to the door, Janice thanked me. Miss Minnie, looked at me with such a tender look and said, "God is going to bless you real good."

He already has, Miss Minnie, He already has!

Neon Daisies

This particular Wednesday was very hectic with extra stops to make, so I began to entertain the idea that Thursday would be better to make my weekly visit to the nursing home.

As I drove through McDonald's to get coffee, I was mentally making my plan and trying to convince myself that tomorrow would be a better day to see Miss Minnie. The view from the drive-thru was that of a supermarket...one with a floral department. I usually try to take Miss Minnie flowers since she's not able to go outside. As I sat waiting for my order, the Lord said, "If you will go and buy the flowers now, before your appointment, you'll go today." So I darted across the four lanes into the supermarket parking lot. Funny how a little monetary investment makes us a little more committed!

The lady in the floral department asked if she could help and I said I was just looking. I kept looking for just the right flower. I had been there for a few minutes when the lady said, "Is this a special occasion?" "No," I said, "I visit a lady in the nursing home and I like to take her a different flower each week, but nothing seems to be exactly what I wanted." "Have you seen these daisies, over here in the case?" She pulled out a bunch of neon colored daisies. They

were electric purple, green, and orange. WOW! They were not what I was looking for, but for some reason, I said I would take them.

I asked her if she would put a ribbon on them while I made out the card. She said, "I sure will and I won't charge you since you are taking them to someone in the nursing home." She began to tell me about a loved one that had recently had a stroke and she was caring for him. She told me she also had elderly parents that needed her and she was just overwhelmed. "But I'm blessed that I can come to work and God is good," she said. "Yes, He is," I said. "What's your name?" "B. J.," she said with a smile. "Well, B. J., I'm going to be praying for you." "Thank you," she said. "I'll be praying for you and the lady you're visiting, too." I walked out of the store shaking my head and pondering the encounter with B.J.

I couldn't wait to present the glow-in-the-dark flowers that B.J. had picked for me to give to Minnie. It's not what I normally would have chosen, but they would certainly brighten up her room! When I checked in at the front desk, I could see many of the residents in the dining room. Some of them had started down the hall in their wheelchairs. As I passed some of them, a gentleman in a bright orange Tennessee cap said, "Boy, those sure are purty flowers." "Thanks," I said, "Would you like to smell them?" "Sure would," he said. I held them to his nose. He smelled them and said, "They sure are purty." I turned to continue to Minnie's room. I got about five steps when the Lord said, "Go back and give him one." I went back to him, pulled out one of the bright orange ones and said, "You need one of these to match your cap!" Money could not buy the smile on that dear man's face. He stuck it behind his ear and happily rolled down the hallway.

All the way down the hall, people would comment on those wild neon flowers! When I walked into Miss Minnie's room, she said, "Ohhh, those are so pretty." Miss Minnie loved to grow flowers in her garden when she was still able. "I've never seen colors like *that* before!" "Well, neither have I," I said with a chuckle, "but I hope you like them." She exclaimed, "I do, they just brighten everything up." Oh, Miss Minnie, if you only knew.

I couldn't have known that day that obeying God and buying flowers in the supermarket would have touched so many people, including me. But that's the way He is, a God of details and a surprise around every corner. He's just waiting to see if we will follow Him with our eyes wide open, waiting with anticipation to see Him at work. When my days are filled with to-dos and I think I'm going to drown in the small stuff, all I have to do is think back on that day. God has every day of our lives cupped in His hand and He cares about each detail…right down to the neon daisies.

Inscribed on the Palm of His Hands

Comprehending the love of God is difficult. In our human state, we can't begin to fully understand the depth of His love. We, parents, may have a small glimpse of what His love is like when we think about the love we have for our children.

I carry a picture of my daughter, Lauren, in my wallet. When I'm at the grocery or the mall, the picture sometimes slips out when I reach for my credit card. Each time it does, it makes me smile. I don't carry the picture because I'm afraid I'll forget what she looks like. I carry it simply because she's mine, I love her, and I love seeing her face when we aren't together. There isn't anything she could ever do that would make me not love her. I would do anything for her. She's part of me and I love her more than life.

In Isaiah 49:16, God says, "See, I have inscribed you on the palms of my hands." Can you comprehend that? Almighty God carries your picture. Does He carry it because he will forget who you are? No! He knew you before you were formed in your mother's womb. He knows everything about you. He has your picture inscribed on the palm of His hand because He loves you.

Maybe you have never felt loved by an earthly father or mother. You may have been rejected by someone you loved and trusted. Perhaps you were abused or cast aside. Rest assured God knows who you are and what you have been through. He hears every cry of your heart. There isn't anything He wouldn't do for you. He is your Heavenly Father and you are so important to Him that He has your picture in the palm of His hand.

Through the Fire

The days we had at home were some of the most hectic I could remember. Fatigue had overcome me and situations and problems were plaguing my thoughts.

We loaded the bus late that night and I fell into bed exhausted, but unable to sleep. I read for a while and finally dozed off, but during the night I awoke several times to those same troubling thoughts. Worry and dread were disrupting my sleep and my peace.

Waking early, I got my Bible and a devotional book and went to the front lounge for a cup of coffee and some quiet time. It only took a few sentences of the first devotional for me to realize that it was especially for me. The first entry related the energy crisis of 1970 to the energy shortage in our lives. Psalm 119 was the scripture reference given to help me understand that my strength is renewed by concentrating on and living according to the Word of God.

The second devotional talked about thankfulness. There are countless blessings we can praise God for daily and yet, we forget our blessings when we are immersed in our problems.

The author of the third devotional related how the fires we go through as Christians are like that of a ceramic object being fired in a kiln. The temperature is gradually raised until the green ware has been fired. Only the hottest fires will produce the most beautiful pieces. We as Christians must go through the fire until God refines us into a beautiful masterpiece of His making.

As I read, I began to feel uplifted. Then I realized something. Each of those messages had been written by three different people at different times, but all three were printed side by side in the same book with the day of the month on them that corresponded with the day in my life when I needed those words of encouragement.

Reflecting on what I had read, I wondered if I would ever learn not to worry but to trust God completely. When our circumstances loom large and we can't see His hand, we must trust His heart. He knows what we need and He has already provided. We can exhaust ourselves with worry or we can trust Him and be at peace.

Matthew 6:34 - "Take therefore no thought for the morrow, for the morrow shall take thought for things of itself. Sufficient unto the day is the evil thereof."

A Date with Ms. Cora

We go to many churches and meet many wonderful people, but some places and people just stand out. Places that just feel like home. Claremore Church of the Nazarene is one of those. We were there for a Christmas concert a few years ago and we fell in love with the people there.

I met a wonderful lady there that night, Cora Merkle. Ms. Cora became my friend and meeting her changed my life. What's so special about Ms. Cora? Well, it's hard to explain, but there are just some people you have a bond with the moment you meet them, and she is one of those people.

Ms. Cora is in her eighties, sharp as a tack, full of God's spirit, and just an absolute joy to be around. One time, when we were in concert there, we were setting up the product display. Roger and Lauren really didn't need my help so I said to Roger, "I'm going to talk to Ms. Cora." I wanted to visit with her a little before the concert. He didn't know that we had struck up a friendship, so he asked me why I wanted to talk to her. I told him that I wanted to talk to her because she knew things that I needed to know. Things that only saints, that have been on this journey a long time, have learned.

This precious lady is a wealth of knowledge and I am so encouraged each time I get to visit with her. She became a teacher after she had raised a family, and she also testified before the state legislature to defend her right to pray in her classroom. She won! She lost her husband several years ago. Most recently, she lost a son. She is a mother, grandmother, and great-grandmother. Most importantly for me, she is a prayer warrior and an encourager.

Did I mention she's a hoot, too! She told me she was the only Cora Merkle in the United States. I asked how she knew that and she said, "Well, I Googled it." She's in her eighties and she googles!!!! She asked me if I was on Facebook and I had to admit that Lauren was, but I wasn't. I asked her if she was and she said, "Of course!" OK, I was a little embarrassed, so I'm on Facebook now. I want to be like her when I'm her age, but I'm already behind.

She has to use a walker now, but her mind and spirit are amazing. Looking into her eyes as she talks about the Lord and hearing her pray is an experience. I always want to sit and talk a little longer with her, but time does not permit. When we have to say goodbye, she always hugs me and says, "I love you, Debra, and remember we have a appointment." She tells me, that when we get to heaven, she will look for me and we will sit and talk for as long as we want. That's a date, Ms. Cora.

If you haven't talked to a "Ms. Cora" lately, I would encourage you to find a mature Christian in your church, community, or in your own family and spend some time with them. They have so much to say that you and I need to hear. If hindsight is 20/20, their perspective is crystal clear. Their wisdom can help us on this journey. Their prayers - priceless!

What Matters Most

A few years ago when were returning home from another long trip, my husband received word that his aunt had passed away and the family wanted us to sing at the graveside service.

A small group of family and friends gathered around the grave on a cold Monday morning. The frozen brown grass crunched beneath our feet as we walked to the small mound of dirt where she would be laid to rest. Everyone shivered from the cold wind that swept through the funeral home tent. The bleakness of the day was a harsh reminder of why we were there.

After we sang, I watched the faces of the grieving family as the pastors each spoke words of comfort. They talked about her life, the kindness she showed to others, and what a faithful wife and mother she had been. They also spoke about her faith in Christ and the fact that they knew she would spend eternity in heaven.

I couldn't help but think, as I stood there, that this is what our lives come down to. Did we know and love Christ? Were we faithful? Did we love and serve others? All of the accomplishments, recognitions, accolades and awards we receive in this life are for

the moment, but how we live our lives is what matters. There were no trophies or medals laid on her grave, just flowers of remembrance from those that loved her.

James 4:14: Whereas you do not know what will happen tomorrow. For what is your life? It is even a vapor that appears for a little time and then vanishes away.

If you knew you only had one day to live, how would you spend it? Would you spend it with family? Maybe mend some relationships that are strained? Would you make sure everything was right between you and God?

This life is not a rehearsal. Today is all we have. Live it like it is your last.

Treasures of the Heart

The old gentleman sat on the beautiful antique sofa in the nearly empty room. Staring into space, his hands trembled slightly on top of his cane, propped between his feet. The faraway look in his eyes told me he really wasn't aware of all the people walking through the house he once called home.

A crowd gathered outside to make their bids, as the auctioneer offered each piece of the old man's life for sale. Still he sat there seeing another time in his mind… a time when the rooms of this house were filled with the laughter of his children. He could almost smell dinner cooking as his loving wife busied herself in the little kitchen.

This was no longer his home. He was now living in a retirement home. Money from the sale of his possessions would help with his expenses.

As the sounds of the auctioneer's chant brought him back to reality, he slowly rose to his feet and stood among the crowd gathered on his front steps. Strangers that had paid a price for a box of his memories one by one loaded them into their vehicles and drove away.

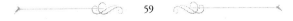

Feeling like an intruder, I left.

I didn't want to see his home left bare of all that had once been important to him. The things that were once important to him were just that, things. Maybe that was how he could watch his possessions being divided among those who gathered at the auction. What still remained were the truly important things in life, a loving family, friends, and the memories of all the wonderful events of a long life well lived.

Those treasures could never be touched by the auctioneer's gavel. They were forever in his heart.

Country Road

One morning, while taking a walk down our little country road, I began to notice things I had paid little attention to before. Most of the time, I would be driving down this little lane in a hurry to get to my errands.

The crisp morning air seemed to awaken all my senses. The beautiful East Tennessee countryside was alive with its early morning sounds. Crickets were chirping in the tall grass, birds were flitting about, roosters were crowing in the distance, and cows were mooing contentedly. The soft breeze rushed past my ears as I walked, butterflies fluttered by me, and I could hear the puttering sounds of a tractor plowing in a field. Even a swarm of gnats and a couple of bees got my attention.

Amid all the busyness of nature, there was a quiet peace in the chorus of its song. I began to wonder how many times I had driven by the familiar sights, going about my business, not taking the time to experience the beauty of it all.

Through these peaceful scenes, God began to show me that my relationship with Him is like that too often. I rush from one

situation or problem to another, breathing a hurried prayer. I begin to get frustrated and discouraged when the answer doesn't come in my time frame. If only I would learn to stop and listen to Him, I would experience that same peace that I felt that day amid the busyness of my life.

If your life is like mine, too busy and too stressful, take the time to seek Him. You'll find peace and contentment in the chaos of life. You may not have a country road to walk down, but His beauty is all around you and you'll find Him wherever you are.

Oh! One more thing, just be thankful you don't have to deal with the gnats and the bees!

You Can't Measure Grace

In October 1989, the San Francisco earthquake dominated the news. Fires, crumbled buildings, collapsed bridges and highways sandwiched together, and people buried in the rubble were horrifying sights. The images on our televisions were unbelievable and as vivid as they were, it didn't compare to what people in that area were actually experiencing. News reporters tried to relay the facts and give the rest of the world some idea of the devastation. Words were inadequate to describe the horror.

One reporter closed his segment by saying that we, who are not affected by the earthquake, look at our televisions, with our hearts going out to the victims and say, "There, but by the grace of God, go I." He then went on to say, "In a situation like this, I don't know if even God's grace could possibly be enough."

I was shocked that the reporter had used a scripture reference, but what a sad statement! Maybe *he* had never experienced the grace of God.

We live by God's grace every day, but in times of life, times of heartache, destruction, and tragedy, Grace is not rationed. When the

secure walls of our lives crumble and fall around us, God's grace is heaped on us according to our need.

Be assured that God's grace cannot be contained or measured. His grace is limitless and His supply is never ever depleted. If we know Him as our Savior, we have access to His never ending supply of amazing Grace!

The Real Stuff

There are always people in need. Whether it's from natural disasters or man-made disasters, our world is full of needy people.

At a discount store, one day, I saw large bins at the end of every checkout. They were for items that people wanted to purchase to donate for the disaster victims of the most recent hurricane.

I loaded a cart with items I thought would be helpful and headed to the checkout. One of the cashiers asked how I wanted it bagged and I told her not to bag it because I was putting it in the bin. She looked at me with a shocked look and said, "All of it?" "Yes," I said. She said, "That's so nice, I can't believe it." I said, "Well, this is the least I can do. I've been very blessed and God expects me to help my neighbor."

My little cart full of items seemed so small in comparison to the magnitude of the disasters. However, if we all do just a little something, it will make a difference.

There's a series of books titled, "Don't Sweat the Small Stuff." We should take that advice, because it's all small stuff. We waste so

much time, energy and money on things that don't really matter. Those who have survived horrific events are happy just to be alive. As I heard a man who had lost everything say, "We are alive and all this is just stuff, it can be replaced."

Now is the time for the church (us) to show God's love. Let's count our blessings and reach out to those in need. We have the "real" stuff they need.

As a Little Child

It's amazing how God uses the simplest things to draw my attention away from my everyday routine to show me more of Himself.

Headed to a store one day to return a purchase, I saw a sight that made me stop and smile. Walking across the parking lot was a mom and her two little girls. The mom had her eye on the girls, while talking on her cell phone. The girls, about three and five, were holding hands and singing.

Yes, Jesus loves me
Yes, Jesus loves me
Yes, Jesus loves me
The Bible tells me so!

Seeing and hearing those little girls made my plans for the day seem so unimportant. Oblivious to anyone watching or listening to them, they were expressing what was in their hearts.

I began to examine my own example. Could someone passing by see what was in my heart? Was my love for Christ visible by my expression or my interaction with others?

Is it any wonder that Jesus used children in his example of what it takes to enter His kingdom? Trusting, pure, open hearts and minds that God can write His song upon. Life may have left its imprint on us, but in Him our hearts, too, can be as a child's.

Everything I Need to Know...

For Mother's Day 1988, my daughter, Lauren, gave me a book titled, "Everything I Need To Know I Learned In Kindergarten." The book by Robert Fulgham is full of nuggets of wisdom that remind us that what we learn early in life are the basics to living fulfilled lives as adults.

Most of us learn very early in life, how to treat others, what to say, and just how to "be." Somewhere along the way, we tend to forget some of those basic principles and have to be reminded how important they really are. My reminder came when I took a field trip with Lauren's kindergarten class. I volunteered to be one of the chaperones for forty (yes, forty) five-year-olds to a hands-on museum.

We boarded the yellow school bus early that morning. Lauren and the two little girls assigned to me were sitting together in one seat. There was no room for me with them. There was only one seat left across the aisle from them and it was right beside two of the cutest little boys I had ever seen. Their name tags said Brandon and Virgil. Brandon was stocky with blond hair and brown eyes and Virgil was wiry with brown hair. I asked them if I could sit with

them. They just smiled so I took that as a yes and sat down. There was something unusual about those little guys, they were QUIET! All of the other children were laughing, talking, and a few fighting, but not these two. They just sat there with their arms around each other's shoulders. They sat like that, not saying a word, until Virgil fell asleep. For the entire bus ride, he made himself comfortable on Brandon. His head was on Brandon's shoulder and his leg was thrown across Brandon's leg. Brandon didn't look very comfortable for the one hour bus ride, but he never complained. There was no pushing, no shoving, no harsh words and no trying to claim his own space. He just sat there holding up his friend. He would look at me and smile a shy smile. It was as if his big brown eyes were saying, "It's alright, he's my buddy."

When bus finally arrived at the museum, Virgil awoke. He sat up and looked at Brandon and smiled shyly, as if he was embarrassed he had been asleep on his friend. Brandon didn't say a word. They just stepped off the bus arm in arm and into a day of fun with each other.

Every time I saw them that day they were still arm in arm having a ball, like best friends do. The example those little guys set that day, without even trying, was a great reminder of what's important in this life; friends helping friends, sharing the load, no questions, no conditions, just love for each other. Everything I need to know I learned in kindergarten. There's a lot of truth in that. Thanks, guys!

Day Care Lesson

As I got off the bus one Monday morning, I realized that my car was in a different parking lot from where the bus was. We had left from the lower parking lot at the church a few days before and I had to walk past the pre-school playground to retrieve my car.

As I neared the fenced-in play area, I could see all the little ones playing. I am a pushover for little kids and I wanted to stop to watch them, but I didn't want the day care workers to be alarmed, so I just kept walking. There is a railroad track on the other side of the church lot and as I passed the kids, I could see and hear a train approaching. The kids were yelling about the choo-choo train. I couldn't help but smile at their excitement.

Just then, over all the noise, I heard one little voice yelling, "Hey, Lady, Hey! Lady!" I turned to look. There was a little boy holding a large plastic ball bat and he was calling me! As I walked back to him, he was pointing at the ball that he had knocked through the fence. I assured the day care workers I was only getting his ball. I retrieved the stray ball and handed it to him through the fence. When he reached out to take the ball from me, I looked into a sweet little face with a runny nose. He smiled and said very sincerely, "Thanks, Lady."

The other little kids then ran to the fence and wanted to talk about the choo-choo that was passing. I walked away with a smile on my face.

I began to think about what had just happened. The scripture that says, "…and a little child shall lead them," came to mind. The little boy trusted someone to help him when he dropped the ball and he knew I was on the side of the fence where the ball lay. The little fellow recognized that there was someone that was close enough to remedy his situation and he didn't hesitate to call out.

I learned a valuable lesson from a small boy with a plastic bat and a runny nose. Too often we drop the ball in our lives and try to fix the situation ourselves only to make matters worse or we just look at the problem through the fence of frustration and wonder how we will ever find an answer, when all we have to do is call on the One closest to us and our problems.

The Bible tells us to "cast your cares upon Him, for He cares for you." The next time you find that you've dropped the ball, just call out. He'll be there!

A Song in the Night

After a concert one evening, a lady told us a story about what our music had meant in her life. The lady said that she and her husband were not able to have children. They had been married for several years and had given up on having a family.

They were worship leaders at their church. After church one night, they received a call from the sheriff, a friend of theirs. He needed them to take three little girls that he had just removed from a home. Their father had murdered their mother and he needed a stable, safe environment for them.

They agreed to take the girls, ages three, six and nine. They took them in and tried to give them a safe, loving home they desperately needed. They began taking them to church and teaching them about Jesus, even taking them to the worship team's rehearsals.

One night after tucking the little girls in bed together, from their bedroom the husband and wife could hear them singing "Triumphantly, the church will rise!" They couldn't believe their ears. The girls had only been to church with them a few times, but they

had picked up the words to one of the Talleys' songs that they had been using in their church.

The couple's commitment to God began to make a difference in the young lives that had been torn apart. A home needing children and children needing a home became the perfect place for God to show His love to both. What Satan meant for harm, God used for good. Those innocent little girl's voices singing in the night, became a song of victory for all.

Three Dollars and Sixty-One Cents in a Ziplog Bag

Was there any better feeling when you were a kid than to have coins jingling in your pocket? Emma found something that gave her a better feeling - giving!

Emma loves the Talleys. According to her family, the Lesters, who are legendary in gospel music, she would probably get on the bus and just go with us. When we are at a concert with them, she comes to our product table and helps us sell our CDs!

Emma is one of the cutest, smartest and sweetest little girls I've ever known. Her mom and dad had been teaching her about tithing, so when Emma's birthday came, Jenny, her mom, explained to Emma that she should tithe on her birthday money. Emma asked, "Who do you give it to?" Jenny told her, "You can give it to your church, to missionaries, singing groups, anyone that is serving the Lord in ministry, or someone in need." Her mom said, "Where would you like to give your tithe, Emma?" Emma thought for a minute and to her mom's surprise she said, "I would like to give it to the Talleys."

Shortly after that, we were with her family in concert. Emma came to our booth for what I thought was one of her usual visits

with us. She came straight to me and handed me a plastic baggie with three dollars and sixty-one cents in change. When I asked her what the money was for she explained that it was her tithe on her birthday money and she wanted us to have it. Her sincerity touched me so that it was all I could do to fight back the tears. I thanked her and told her I would like to use that money to help some boys and girls at a children's home that we supported. I told her it would help get them things they need like food and clothes. She smiled from ear to ear and said, "That's a good idea!" I gave her a big hug and told her I was proud of her and Jesus was proud of her.

Emma didn't have any problem letting go of something that would have brought her pleasure; she chose to be obedient to God and help those in need. Through the teaching of her great parents, she knows that it is more blessed to give than receive. She's learned a valuable principle that God expects us to give back to Him from His blessings to us.

I couldn't part with the baggie, so I tucked it in my desk drawer. I sent the equivalent of her offering to the children's home along with my contribution. Each time I open the desk drawer and see my little friend's offering, I'm reminded that blessings that come in small packages sometimes have the greatest impact!

Do You Know Jesus?

Anyone with children or anyone that's ever known a child can agree that you never know what will come out of their mouths next. They aren't worried about what someone will think. They don't get political correctness. (Thank goodness.) If they have a question, they just blurt it out. The purity of their hearts and their curiosity make it such a joy to be around them. With this in mind, meet Jules!

We were scheduled to sing at a church in North Carolina where the pastor and his family were friends of ours. We hadn't seen him and his family in some time. Two of his children were grown and moved away, but his two younger daughters were still at home. They had grown so much that we hardly recognized them.

His youngest was five years old and met us at the door when we arrived. Jules was a very curious little girl, as most five-year-olds are, and asked question after question. The inquisition went on for some time while we were setting up our product display and continued even when we went to the auditorium to sound check.

We got a kick out of all the things she could come up with. I really think the police department in their town could use her. She

would be a great interrogator. As Lauren was doing her sound check, our little friend began to question me about the ear monitors we wear. I explained that we wore them so we could hear the music and ourselves while we sing. She then said, "Can I wear it?" I told her it was made just for my ear and wouldn't fit hers. "Oh," she said, "It's for big people's ears." We then began to discuss the difference in big people's ears and little people's ears.

Right in the middle of our talk about ears, she looked at me and said, "Do you know Jesus?" I said, "Yes, Jules, I do, do you?" She said very confidently, "Yes, he lives in my heart." "Me too," I said. Without missing a beat, she went right back to talking about big people's ears and little people's ears.

I was a bit surprised by Jules' directness, but she got right to the point, no beating around the bush. Mark 10:15 says, "…Whoever does not receive the kingdom of God as a little child will by no means enter it." I'll get right to the point, do you know Jesus? If so, when was the last time you asked a friend, loved one, or a complete stranger that question? If not, would you like to know Jesus? You can pray a simple prayer of salvation right now.

Lord Jesus, I realize that I am a sinner. I ask you to forgive my sin and come into my heart. I receive your free gift of salvation and ask you to be my Lord and Savior. Thank you for loving me and dying for me.

Humility and Lice

Humility is a virtue that is best learned and lived. You will certainly learn humility if you have children.

A friend of ours was asked by his young son what the word humble meant. After stammering around for a while in search of an answer, our friend said, "Well, son, humble means, uh...very humble."

I know how he felt. It's hard to explain it to a child. When, our daughter, Lauren, was a little girl, she asked me if I was humble. Now that's a tough one. If you say yes, then chances are you aren't truly humble. If you say no, then you have that unanswerable question to deal with - why not? You can't declare humility. You, hopefully, learn it through life lessons and I had a lesson in humility not long after Lauren asked me the question.

One day Lauren and I were in the pharmacy section of a discount store. She was minding our cart while I was looking for pain reliever just a few steps away. There were three ladies waiting in line for their prescriptions not far from where we were. Suddenly, Lauren said in a voice loud enough to be heard on the other side of the store,

"MOM! Come here quick, look at my arm!" I looked toward her and could see she was ok. Before I could get to her, she said loudly, "What is this on my arm, LICE?" The ladies burst into laughter, either at her or maybe they had had similar experiences and were laughing that it was my turn to be publicly embarrassed by my child. I tried to explain to Lauren that the small white bumps were not lice and that they would go away. I wasn't sure I convinced her but she stopped yelling. My face eventually returned to its normal color, but only after I left that aisle and moved to another part of the store. Why couldn't she have asked me that in the privacy of our home? Wouldn't I have learned the same lesson there? Uh....no! A crowded store, little white bumps, and one small girl had suddenly clarified the meaning of the word "humility" for me.

Occasionally I hear a small voice ask me, "Are you humble?" Well, I still can't answer that one, but, hopefully, I'm getting there one small bump at a time!

The Worst Place

"This is the worst place!" That's what Lauren heard her mom say half joking, half serious. The little town, we were to sing in at a county fair, wasn't exactly a hub of activity. "It must be a hundred degrees," I told my niece, who was visiting with us. The only motel in town was certainly no Hilton and we had walked what seemed like a mile to find a restaurant. At the fairgrounds, we sang under a big tent and had to compete with the noise of the rides just to be heard.

At every opportunity, Lauren and Beth would take off for the Ferris wheel and other rides. No record was kept of how much they consumed from the concessions stands. After the last concert had ended, we shook the sawdust from our feet, climbed aboard the bus, and headed for the next town. Not even aware that Lauren had heard my earlier remarks, I was settling back, enjoying my nice cool room on the bus, when Lauren burst through the door and said, "Mom, I didn't think this was the worst place, I thought it was the BEST!" I was just a bit embarrassed by my comments and a little convicted that she had overheard me complain.

I guess when you are six years old, traveling with your parents who love you, tagging along with your twelve-year-old cousin whom

you idolize, riding rides at the county fair until you're hot, sticky and blissfully exhausted, eating hot dogs and drinking Mello Yello until you are about to pop, and playing Crazy Eights beating the socks off your Mom: that little town probably did seem like it was the best place in the world.

Maybe the world just looks different through the eyes of a child. And maybe, just maybe, Mom needs to get a good look at things through *her* eyes once in a while.

My Favorite Christmas

Each December, I'm reminded of past Christmases. My favorite Christmas is the year our daughter, Lauren, was born.

We lived in North Carolina at the time and normally would be going to visit my family in Kentucky, which was about a twelve hour drive. We then would spend a few days with Roger's family in East Tennessee on our way back home. Since she was born two weeks before Christmas, we decided we just couldn't make the long trip to Kentucky with a new baby. A wise decision! We were, however, going to drive the shorter distance to Roger's parents, so we decided we would exchange our gifts to each other before we left.

Roger went to the mall and bought a large red felt stocking with a white furry cuff at the top with her name written in gold glitter! We put her tiny little body down in the stocking, feet first of course. Then we propped her up in a chair and took her picture. It's too cute!

After dinner that night, we wrapped her in a blanket and laid her under the tree with all the gifts. Roger and I sat on the floor and began to unwrap our gifts to each other. I would hand him a gift and he would open it, look at her, and cry. He would hand me a gift

and I would open it, look at her, and cry. That continued until all our gifts were opened.

I really can't remember a thing I received that year, not because I didn't love them or appreciate them, but because nothing could compare to our little gift God had given us lying under the tree.

I wonder if Mary felt much the same when Jesus was born. As she wrapped her baby in swaddling clothes and laid him in a manger, she must have praised God and marveled at the miracle. Wise men came and brought priceless gifts to honor Jesus birth, but nothing could compare to the gift God had given her.

Each Christmas as you open your gifts, give thanks for your blessings. Remember with each one you unwrap, you are celebrating the greatest gift ever given to man. Jesus Christ, our Lord!

Barbie and Compassion

Traditions are a big part of our Christmas season. When our daughter, Lauren, was a little girl, we started a new tradition that taught her a lesson about giving.

We were in a mall shopping for Christmas presents when she noticed a different kind of Christmas tree. The branches of the Angel Tree were full of cards with the names, ages, and requests from boys and girls less fortunate. Lauren asked what those cards were. I explained that those were wishes for gifts from children that might not get anything for Christmas. The idea was to choose a card and purchase a gift for that child and return it to the tree. Before I could suggest that we take one, Lauren said, "Oh, Mommy, could we choose one and buy a gift?" Of course, I was thrilled that she had suggested it first.

She chose a little girl about her age with the same love for Barbie dolls. We went to the toy store and made our purchase. At that time, you were to return it wrapped with the card attached. We went to the gift wrap station and it was so crowded that it would take too long to get our gift wrapped. We went to the card store and I bought a sheet of Christmas paper and tape. Since there was such a crowd and no

convenient place to wrap a package, we sat down in the floor of the mall and began to wrap the Barbie. Using Lauren's little fingers to hold the paper while I taped, we finally finished our project. Lauren took the gift and card to the attendant at the tree. We stood there for a minute looking at all those cards hanging from the tree. I was thinking that I wished we could do more when Lauren looked up at me and said, "We shared, didn't we, Mom?"

I knew at that moment that she had grasped what I so wanted her to learn, that it is more blessed to give than to receive. She would have a great Christmas that year. She would receive most of the things on her Christmas list, but the greatest thing she would receive was not on her list. She had learned about compassion. Her world had expanded to include those less fortunate. Her Christmas spirit would be more about giving now and not just getting.

My little girl that placed her gift at the Angel Tree all those years ago is now a married woman, and still continues the tradition to this day. When she has children, I know she will teach them the same lesson. I can only hope I get to be there and see another little one's heart expand to include others!

Thirteen Days and Counting

Do you ever feel a little bah-humbug at Christmas?

Have you seen the commercial with the little girl counting the days until Christmas by watching the countdown ornament on her tree? Her anxious anticipation is almost contagious.

I can remember that feeling as a child. It was almost unbearable, the wait to see what would be under the tree on Christmas morning. We would always get up way too early for our poor, tired parents, but when our eyes popped open, there was no way we could stay in bed.

As my daughter was growing up, I experienced that breathless excitement through her, and I became the poor, tired parent! It was almost impossible to drag myself out of bed before she got up on Christmas morning. I would try to get up and get the camera ready to take pictures of her coming down the stairs before she got up.

My joy was still there for the Christmas season, but it was no longer about what was under the tree. It was seeing the excitement and joy on her face. I wouldn't trade those moments for all the gifts in the world.

That's what happens as we grow and mature. Christmas becomes less about what we want and more about what we can give to others, at least it should. I like and appreciate gifts as much as anyone, but it's still true that it is more blessed to give than to receive. For me, the blessing is not a reward of giving, but the act of giving itself. The blessing I get from giving gives me that excitement and joy that I felt as a child.

Right now, there are thirteen days until Christmas. Oh wait, it's twelve now. Well you get the idea. If you find yourself dreading the holidays, you have some time to capture that joy.

Apart from the gifts you will give to your family and friends, there are many charities and organizations that need our help at this time of year. You may even have a neighbor or family member that just needs a visit from you. Some of the best gifts don't need to be wrapped.

Whether it's your time, money, or beautifully wrapped gifts, there are many ways to reach out to others with love and compassion. Not just at Christmas, but throughout the year. After all, isn't that what Christ did? He came as a baby in a manger to give all He was, for our sake. We can't save the world this Christmas, but we can make a difference in one life at a time.

Still feeling a little bah-humbug? Go ahead. Start your countdown to indescribable joy!!

The Christmas Play

Driving home one evening, past a local country church, I noticed their parking lot was unusually full and I suspected they were having their Christmas program.

It didn't take long to confirm that I was right. Coming through the front door at a fast pace was a teenage shepherd dressed in a bed sheet with a towel on his head. It looked as if he was trying to escape, but the church was small and I'm sure the shepherds and wise men were entering from outside. I got a chuckle out of it and then it reminded me of the first Christmas play of my daughter, Lauren.

Lauren was two years old when she first appeared on stage at the Shady Grove Free Will Baptist Church Christmas pageant. She was chosen to open the event since she couldn't quite memorize a part. She was supposed to walk out on stage as the homemade curtain was pulled open and say her lines. We rehearsed over and over and over, "Hi, you are welcome to our Christmas play!" She knew the lines perfectly. I would say several times a day, "Lauren, say your lines." She would immediately reply with so much fervor, "HI, YOU ARE WECOME TO OWR CHWISMAS PWAY." Rs and Ls were still a problem. It was sooooo cute!

On the night of the play, she had on her Christmas outfit, a little white ruffled blouse, plaid skirt, red knee socks, black patent Mary Janes. Again, too cute. She was positioned behind the homemade curtain and I was behind the organ, you know, just in case. As the curtains parted and the light hit her, she froze. I kept prompting her. but as she realized there were lots of people watching her, she started backing up, shaking her head, saying "uh-uh, uh-uh, uh-uh!" She ran to me behind the organ. She received laughter and applause, I think, for just being cute! The play went on as planned, albeit without a proper welcome.

Whether you find the shepherds running out the door, the baby playing Jesus having a meltdown in the manger, a real animal in the play leaving a present of its own, or the cute little girl welcoming you to the program backing up in fright, I hope you will enjoy the season and make some wonderful memories of your own. Oh, be sure to go to the Christmas pageant! It will definitely make your Christmas merry.

Hometown Heroes

At the beginning of the Gulf War, I witnessed a sight that has stayed with me for years.

I was driving into town to do my errands one morning. A few miles out of town, the traffic slowed to a snail's pace. I assumed it was road work or an accident ahead. As I topped a hill, I could see the reason for the crawling traffic.

There on the lawn of the National Guard Armory were a couple hundred people. Men, women, boys and girls were waving American flags and walking down the hill as they watch buses loaded with their loved ones pull out onto the highway. They stood waving and crying until the buses were out of sight. I'll admit there was a lump in my throat thinking about what these families were sacrificing for me. I began to pray for those soldiers and the families they were leaving behind.

About eighteen months later, signs all over town on banks, churches, and businesses were welcoming the 278th and the 190th National Guard units home. Yellow ribbons decorated every utility pole throughout the town all the way out to the Armory. There were

hundreds of welcome home signs stuck in the ground there and in yards all over town. Our town even had a welcome home parade down Main Street. Our hometown heroes were given a homecoming deserving of their service.

But, there is another sign in our town. This marker, on the courthouse lawn, lists the names of the soldiers that didn't return to a parade. They are our fallen heroes.

We are blessed beyond measure in our town and in our country. Men and women willingly put their lives on hold and leave their families to defend our way of life. Many even sacrifice their lives because this American ideal is so precious.

May we be genuinely thankful for our blessings. May we express our gratitude to those who have given their all to defend our freedom, and may we reach out to those whose loved ones have paid the ultimate sacrifice.

Who Will Pray?

In the United States alone, there are enough tragic events, natural disasters, and political and social mayhem to fill hours and hours of video highlights in the news. We shake our heads at all the craziness and go on with our lives.

If there is a tornado, hurricane, flood, or catastrophic event in part of our country, we pray and maybe even respond to the need. As long as it doesn't affect our lives directly, we tend to forget, in time, and go about our lives until the next big event. Don't get me wrong, I'm not judging. I'm confessing that I do the same thing.

We often offer up prayers for our nation at memorials and national observances, and in time of crisis, but is prayer for this country part of our daily lives? Often, I feel very helpless. I'm just one person. What possible difference could I make in this chaotic world?

The Bible has the answer. James 5:16 - The effectual, fervent prayer of a righteous man avails much. II Chronicles 7:14 - If my people who are called by my name will humble themselves, and pray and seek my face, and turn from their wicked ways, then I will hear

from heaven, and will forgive their sin, and heal their land. (Note the four conditions to the response). Jeremiah 33:3 - Call to Me, and I will answer you, and show you great and mighty things, which you do not know.

Pray or prayer is mentioned 259 times in the Bible, so it must be important to our lives. If we would seriously commit to praying for our homes, loved ones, communities, country and our world, I believe we would see God work in miraculous ways, not only in our world, but in our own hearts and lives.

We have a song titled "Who Will Pray," that is a call to action for all of us to pray. I believe that we are at a point in time that we can no longer afford to take prayer lightly. We must get serious about prayer to see change.

Jesus, in the Garden of Gethsemane, asked his disciples to watch and pray. When He found them sleeping, he asked, "Could you not tarry one hour?" Can we not tarry one hour for our nation, our churches, our communities, and our families? One hour in prayer could be the turning point for our lives and the life of our nation.

We may feel inadequate on our own, but together we can pray and see "great and mighty things" happen. Let's band together to make a difference.

This is America!

In 2009, we were privileged to be a part of the local Veteran's Day Celebration in our hometown. Approximately, twenty five hundred people were in attendance for the festivities.

Even though the rain was pouring outside, people braved the bad weather to honor our local veterans. The combined marching bands of the two local high schools did an incredible job of playing patriotic songs for the parade of soldiers from every war since World War II. The local Boy Scout troops also took part in the parade. One of our U.S. representatives spoke, and The Talleys and Squire Parsons sang.

This was a community event, but not one official told us we could not sing gospel songs. As a matter of fact, that's why we were asked to be there. As Christian music was sung and played, people clapped their hands and praised the Lord in the Expo center. We honored our country and our Lord.

As I stood there and watched the soldiers, the flag, and listened to the songs of our country and our faith, my heart swelled with pride and I kept thinking that this is what America truly is, not politics and agendas.

America is pride in our men and women who sacrifice their lives to protect the freedoms we enjoy every day. America is communities coming together for each other all across our nation when there is a need. America is looking beyond ourselves and reaching out to the less fortunate all across the globe. America is the privilege of being able to express ourselves in our thoughts, speech, and beliefs. America's honor is being maligned in our world today, but even with its faults, it's still the place that people dream of coming to for a better life.

My nephew is a Marine. My father is a World War II Navy veteran. We are America because young men and women risk their lives to protect and defend our nation, and old men lived to tell their stories of the battles that have preserved our freedom for generations.

While seated at a very crowded restaurant one day, I noticed a group of soldiers come in and sit at a table just across the aisle. They seemed so young. I could have been their mother.

My heart kept telling me to walk over and say thank you for their service, but I thought there was too many people to do it discreetly. As we got up to leave, I decided that they were brave enough to serve us, I should be bold enough to say thank you in a crowded place. I walked over to those young men and expressed my gratitude to them and left.

Later that night at the concert, a man came up to me and said he was in the restaurant and heard me say thank you to the soldiers. He said that it made him realize that he needed to do the same. I don't know what impact, if any, my actions made on the young soldiers, but saying thank you was good for me.

Let us never forget who we are, where we have come from, and those that have sacrificed to defend our freedom. It's the surest way to preserve the nation we love.

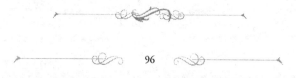

Auld Lang Syne

Do you know what auld lang syne means? Polls show that 85% of us don't know the meaning of the song or know the words. Most of us are familiar with the Guy Lombardo orchestra version that we often hear on New Year's Eve. The first verse and chorus are sung around the world at the stroke of midnight to "ring out the old and ring in the new." Many will sing the song with glasses of spirits held high and never know what they are singing.

The song's origin is dated back to 1711 as a poem by James Watson. In 1799, the Scottish poet Robert Burns used the original and added to it his own verses. The tune then was attributed to an old man that sang the song to him. This is probably not the tune we sing today, but no one is quite sure where the current tune came from.

I never knew what Auld Lang Syne meant exactly. I thought it had something to do with old acquaintances and drinking, which is why we didn't sing it. The line "we'll take a cup of kindness" is the Scottish influence, but it was originally sung in front of St. Paul's Church in Scotland at midnight on New Year's Eve.

The song has a beautiful meaning, though. It ask the question, "Should we forget the relationships and memories of days gone by." Some interpretations say simply, "Let's remember those we love and keep the past in our memories." There may be those that would rather not look back on the past year. Some things may be too painful to remember, but for Christians, we can look back on even the hardest of times and see God's faithfulness. He has been with us every one of the last 365 days and will be with us in the next. His promise is "He will never leave us or forsake us." So no matter what the new year holds for us, because He lives, we can face tomorrow.

This New Year's Eve, whatever you are singing, remember to hold your loved ones close, give thanks for the days gone by, and know that God is holding your future.

Debra Talley

Time

Time is a strange thing to me. It's as illusive as tomorrow and as intangible as yesterday. It can't be banked or borrowed. We use the phrase, "time stood still" to describe some moment in our lives. A measure of time that was so important that we would like to freeze it so our minds can absorb it. However, time never stands still. There is a line in an old song that says "If I could save time in a bottle…" The writer then goes on to tell what he would do with the time he captured. Older folks always say that the older you get the faster time goes by. I'm finding that to be more true with each passing year.

We are the most aware of time when we are in a hurry or when we are reflecting on it. It's measured in seconds, minutes, hours, days, weeks, months, years, decades, centuries, and millennia.

The past can determine our present and our present can determine our future. We can't relive our past and neither can we project ourselves into the future. So how do we make the most of our days? We live in the present. Oh, I know we do this without even thinking about it! Maybe that's the issue. We don't think to much about the time that is today. Are you regretting the past? Fearing the future? The present is filled with moments. We only have this moment to live out. Do we put this moment on hold hoping for something better or do we savor this moment and the next and the next?

My friend was on a trip with her young son and was trying to get an eight year old to appreciate all the memories she was trying to make with him. I gathered he wasn't too impressed with all the plans she had made, videos she had taken of him, and sunrises she had eagerly wanted to share with him. He just wanted to enjoy the trip. As she shared with me her frustration at his indifference, I told her maybe she should not be so consumed with making memories that she missed the moments!

Moments are fleeting, but they are precious, because that's all we have. Not yesterday or tomorrow. Just now. It's hard to fully appreciate every moment, they go by so fast. But, couldn't we slow down enough to let at least some moments catch up with us? I wonder what would happen. Maybe we would actually be present in our own lives. We could enjoy our "now." Many of us work so hard at investing in our futures that our now is bankrupt. Whatever your moments hold for you today, be grateful and give thanks for each one. It's all you have.

About the Author

In gospel music circles, few names are as admired and respected as Debra Talley. Born and raised in Clinton, KY, her singing career began in church at an early age. Her career has now spanned almost four decades.

She travels over one hundred fifty days a year with her husband, Roger, and daughter, Lauren Talley Alvey, as The Talleys.

Her golden alto voice is one of the most recognized in the industry. Her warmth and her humble personality have endeared her to audiences throughout her extensive career.

When she is not traveling, singing, and writing, Debra loves to be home where she enjoys cooking, reading, sewing, and home projects. She and her husband, Roger, reside in East Tennessee. They are avid Tennessee Lady Vols fans and attend as many home games as possible.

With numerous industry awards to her credit, she now adds author to her list of accomplishments. The most important thing to her is living a life dedicated to God and making a difference in the lives of those around her.